LEARNING PYTHON

The Ultimate Guide to Learning How to Develop Applications for Beginners with Python Programming Language Using Numpy, Matplotlib, Scipy and Scikit-learn

Samuel Hack

Download the Audio Book Version of This Book for FREE

If you love listening to audio books on-the-go, I have great news for you. You can download the audio book version of this book for FREE just by signing up for a FREE 30-day audible trial! See below for more details!

AUDIBLE TRIAL BENEFITS

As an audible customer, you will receive the below benefits with your 30-day free trial:

- FREE audible book copy of this book
- After the trial, you will get 1 credit each month to use on any audiobook
- Your credits automatically roll over to the next month if you don't use them
- Choose from Audible's 200,000 + titles
- Listen anywhere with the Audible app across multiple devices
- Make easy, no-hassle exchanges of any audiobook you don't love
- Keep your audiobooks forever, even if you cancel your membership
- And much more

For Audible US:
https://www.audible.com/pd/B07Y5QMKKN/?source_code=AUDFPWS02 23189MWT-BK-ACX0-165151&ref=acx_bty_BK_ACX0_165151_rh_us
For Audible UK:
https://www.audible.co.uk/pd/B07Y5PFNV9/?source_code=AUKFrDlWS 02231890H6-BK-ACX0-165151&ref=acx_bty_BK_ACX0_165151_rh_uk
For Audible FR:
https://www.audible.fr/pd/B07Y5Q2JHM/?source_code=FRAORWS0223 18903B-BK-ACX0-165151&ref=acx_bty_BK_ACX0_165151_rh_fr
For Audible DE:
https://www.audible.de/pd/B07Y5Q13SB/?source_code=EKAORWS0223 189009-BK-ACX0-165151&ref=acx_bty_BK_ACX0_165151_rh_de

TABLE OF CONTENTS

Introduction

Congratulations on purchasing *Learning Python,* and thank you for doing so.

The following chapters will discuss all of the different options and things that you need to know when it comes to working with the Python coding language. There may be a ton of other coding languages out there, all with their proponents and those who will only ever use this kind of coding language for their needs. But for many coders, whether they are just learning how to code for the first time or they are more advanced and have been doing their coding for a very long time, Python is one of the best options to work with.

This guidebook is going to delve a bit into the basics of working with the Python language and will explore more about what Python is all about. We will start out this guidebook with a good introduction to what Python is, some of the benefits of working with this language, and even some of the basic parts that come with a Python code so that anyone, even a beginner, will be ready to take it to the next level when we work on some of the examples of writing code later.

From there, we are going to explore what it means when we say that Python is an OOP language, and how the classes and objects work in this language. We will also look at some of the other neat things that you are able to do within the Python language including how to write loops, working with the decision control statements, how to raise an exception, and even how to work with inheritances and regular expressions.

The end of this guidebook is going to move on from some of the basics of writing codes in Python and will delve a bit deeper into what you are able to do with some of the Python libraries. We will focus mainly on what is possible with the Scikit-Learn library but will explore some of the other options when you are ready to take your coding to the next level.

There are so many benefits that come with working on the Python coding language, and so many people love working with this to help them create any kind of program. When you are ready to learn how to make this coding language work the best for your needs and you want to learn some of the different parts so that you can start writing your own codes, make sure to check out this guidebook to get started.

There are plenty of books on this subject on the market, thanks again for choosing this one! Every effort was made to ensure it is full of as much useful information as possible. Please enjoy!

Chapter 1: What is Python?

There are a lot of different coding languages that you are able to work with. The option that you choose is often going to depend on the amount of experience that you have along with what you are trying to do inside the code that you want to right. Some coding languages are going to be a bit more advanced, some are going to work best with some websites, and some are going to work best with one kind of operating system or another. Each of these coding languages is going to provide you with some benefits, and choosing one as a beginner is going to seem like a big challenge for a beginner.

Even though there are a ton of options that come with coding languages, you will find that one of the best options, whether you are a beginner or more advanced in coding, is Python. You will find that the Python language is simple to use, while still allowing you to really work on some high-quality coding, without posing all of the challenges to a beginner. In fact, this coding language is often one that is recommended to those who are brand new to coding and have never been able to work with any kind of coding in the past.

There are a lot of things to love about this kind of language. It is easy to work with and learn, even with all of the power that comes with it. You will be able to write codes in no time, and the wording is in English, unlike some of the other options you can choose out there, which make it a bit easier to work with overall. And the other tools, like having some good libraries, help from many other people in the coding world, open source programming that is free and more makes it the perfect option when you are first getting started with this kind of language.

You will find that there are a lot of benefits that come with the Python language. The first benefit that we are going to take a look at is the support libraries. You will find that just by opening up the Python language, there are a lot of options available in the library. And you can look at third-party libraries and extensions that can easily be added to this coding language.

This is a great option for you, whether you are a beginner or more advanced with your coding. It is going to provide you with a lot of options on what you are able to do with your coding and can make things easier. You will be able to add in a lot of classes, objects, and functions in this, and that can make life so much easier overall. You can always work just with the libraries and extensions that come with the Python language when you download it, or you can go through and add in some third party libraries to this if you would like some special features and more to work on your codes.

There are a lot of different benefits that are going to help you to really see results with the Python code. You will first enjoy that this is going to be a great option because of all the options that work in the library. The library is going to have a lot of neat codes and options that you are able to work with, that makes it easier for the beginner to get started.

There are also a lot of different options that you can do with this code. It has a ton of power behind it, which many beginners worry that they are not going to be able to learn how to work with this. You will be able to do a ton of things when it comes to this language, whether you have been able to code or not. And it is easily comparable to a lot of the more complicated coding languages that are out there. It may have included a lot of power with it, but it was going to be easy enough to help you to make any code that you want, even if you are a big beginner and have never worked on this kind of coding before.

There is also a large community to use when you are working with Python. There are a lot of programmers, whether they are brand new to coding or have been doing it for some time, which will use this coding language. This allows you to ask questions and find a lot of communities that you are able to work with and see results. This makes it so much easier for you to see how to do things, to get your questions answered, and so much more.

How to install the Python language

Now that we know a bit more about using the Python language and why it is going to be a good tool to work with, it is time to move on and figure out what steps you need to follow in order to make sure that the Python language is set up and installed on your computer. You want to make sure that you get the Python code set up on the computer in the proper manner, to ensure that you are able to write out some of the codes that you need, without ending up with any struggles or errors along the way.

Before you, as a programmer will be able to look through some of the other parts of this guidebook and before you are able to work with writing some of your own codes, you need to make sure that the Python language is set up and that you are able to set up the interpreter. Installation for Python is going to be depending on the kind of operating system that is on your computer, along with the installation source that you would like to work with. You do get a few choices when you pick out the source of downloading the Python code, but to make things as easy as possible, we are going to work with www.python.org.

This is why we are going to spend some time looking at the way that you will need to install the Python interpreter and the steps that you can use based on the operating system that you are going to use it on. Let's divide up this chapter and look at some of the different steps that you can use to make this work for you.

How to install the Mac OS X

If you plan to use the Python coding language on a Mac operating system when you are ready to install the system, you will find that the Python 2 version should already be on the system, even before you do anything else with it. The exact version of this though is often going to depend on when you got the computer and how old it is. If you are curious about which Python version is on your computer, you just need to open up the prompt for commands and type in the code "python – V." This will list out the version number of Python that is already on the computer so you can decide if that is the one that you want to use or not.

Now, you may decide that you want to use a newer version of Python and even with Python 3. There are a lot of people who would like to change this up, and there are a few steps that you are able to work with, in order to get it all set up into any version of Python that you would like to use. We want to work with Python 3 to make things easier. To check out if the computer has a Python 3 installation on your system, you first need to make sure that you open up the terminal app that we had from before, and type in the code "python3 – V" to see if it is there.

The default with the Mac system, unless you or someone else already installed it on your system, is that Python 3 will not be found on your computer. This means that we need to do the work to get it installed on your computer by visiting the website of www.python.org. This is often the easiest place to start because it is going to include all of the different parts that you need to make the code work. This means that it is going to include all of the tools that are needed the IDLE, the shell, and the interpreter.

Being able to run the IDLE and the shell with this language is going to depend on the specific version of the Python that you want to work with, and you can even choose base on your own preferences when you are doing the coding. The two commands that work the best to make this happen will include:

For Python 2.X just type in "Idle"
For Python 3.X, just type in "idle3"

As we brought up before, when you actually stop and take the time to install and download your Python 3 program on an operating system with Mac, you will need to install the IDLE at the same time to make sure that you are able to do the codes. If you get Python from python.org, you will be fine, and everything will be installed at the same time. If you decide to install this from somewhere else, you will need to check that all of the parts are found there or not, and then install what doesn't seem to show up.

Installing Python on the Windows system

Now, it is possible for you to download your Python program on a Windows System rather than on a Mac system. You may want to make sure that it is added onto this kind of computer, and you will have to go through a few steps. Windows has its own coding language already found on it, which means that it is not going to have the Python code on it. You will need to go through the right steps in order to get it on the system. It will work just fine on a Windows computer, but you do need to take the steps necessary to get it all installed on your computer.

When you are ready to work with adding the Python language on a computer that has Windows on it, you will need to go through and come up with the right variables for the environment that are needed so that you can bring up the Python commands, just using the prompt. The steps that are needed to help you get the Python code set up on a Windows computer includes:

To set this up, you need to visit the official Python download page and grab the Windows installer. You can choose to do the latest version of Python 3, or go with another option. By default, the installer is going to provide you with the 32-bit version of Python, but you can choose to switch this to the 64-bit version if you wish. The 32-bit is often best to make sure that there aren't any compatibility issues with the older packages, but you can experiment if you wish.

Now right click on the installer and select "Run as Administrator." There are going to be two options to choose from. You will want to pick out "Customize Installation." On the following screen, make sure all of the boxes under "Optional Features" are clicked and then click to move on. While under Advanced Options," you should pick out the location where you want Python to be installed. Click on Install. Give it some time to finish and then close the installer.

Next, set the PATH variable for the system so that it includes directories that will include packages and other components that you will need later. To do this, use the following instructions:

Open up the Control Panel. Do this by clicking on the taskbar and typing in Control Panel. Click on the icon.

Inside the Control Panel, search for Environment. Then click on Edit the System Environment Variables. From here, you can click on the button for Environment Variables.

Go to the section for User Variables. You can edit the PATH variable that is there, or you can create one.

If there isn't a variable for PATH on the system, then create one by clicking on New. Make the name for the PATH variable and add in the directories that you want. Click on close all the control Panel dialogs and move on.

Now you can open up your command prompt. Do this by clicking on Start Menu, then Windows System, and then Command Prompt. Type in "python." This is going to load up the Python interpreter for you.

After you have been able to go through some of these steps, don't worry the steps are easier than you would think, you will be able to go through and open up the programming for Python. You can then use this in any manner that you want, just like you would with any other system. You can then take some time to set up the interpreter in the manner that you would like, write out the codes that we have in this guidebook and more, and create any kind of program that you would like.

Installing Python on a Linux operating system

We can also take some time to install the Python language on a Linux operating system. This is an operating system that a lot of people like to work with because it is simple and allows you to do a lot of things that you may not have been able to do on other programs. It is often seen as one of the easiest operating systems to use when it comes to downloading and working with the Python language, so if you are still on the fence about which operating system to use, then it may be worth your time to work with Linux.

The steps to get the Python coding language on your computer will be a bit different compared to some of the other operating systems that we have talked about before. Some of the codes and the steps that you will need to use in order to get the Python coding language, and all of the things that go with it, installed on your computer include:

$ python3 - - version

If you are on Ubuntu 16.10 or newer, then it is a simple process to install Python 3.6. You just need to use the following commands:

$ sudo apt-get update
$ sudo apt-get installs Python3.6

If you are relying on an older version of Ubuntu or another version, then you may want to work with the deadsnakes PPA, or another tool, to help you download the Python 3.6 version. The code that you need to do this includes:

```
$ sudo apt-get installs software-properties-common
$ sudo add-apt repository ppa:deadsnakes/ppa
# suoda apt-get update
$ sudo apt-get installs python3.6
```

While this does include a bit more code writing than what you are going to see with some of the other operating systems, for the most part, the different distributions of Linux are going to already have Python 3 on them. You can double check to see if this is true. Sometimes the Python 3 may not be on this system for one reason or another, or you will want to go through and update the system a bit to make sure it has what you would like, and you can do that using the codes that we wrote above.

A look at the interpreter

Before we dive into some of the different codes that you are able to work with when it comes to Python, we need to understand a bit more about some of the parts that come with the language, and the things that you need to include with it to see the best results. We need to first start with the interpreter for Python. The standard installation that you are able to receive when you download this language from www.python.org is going to have the interpreter, along with all of the other parts that are needed in order to start some of your codings. This means that all of the files, the interpreter, the licensing, the documentation, and more are all going to be found in the download that you need.

The three files that will come with the Python download are going to include the IDLE, the shell, and the interpreter. First, let's take a look at the interpreter for Python. This is something that is important to work with because it is the part of the program that can execute any and all codes that you write. The interpreter is going to take in all of the lines of code that you write and can send them as instructions to be read. It will do the job of processing the orders that you tell it, and executing the code on the screen.

Once you have a good interpreter in place, it is time to work with the Python IDLE. The IDLE is going to stand for integrated development and learning environment. You want to have this in place because it is going to be responsible for holding onto each and every tool that you need when it is time to create some new programs with Python. The right IDLE will hold onto the options for debugging your code, the text editor, and the shell that you will like to use when writing your codes. The IDLE can have a lot of features, or you can keep it basic, and that is going to depend on your own preferences along with which version of Python you would like to use.

If you go to the www.python.org version and decide to download that for your needs, then the IDLE is going to come with that download. However, you may notice that there are a lot of third party options that you can choose if you want to work with a different kind of IDLE in the process. If you are going to be writing a specific type of code for your program or you would like to have some different features with your IDLE, then you can download those at this time and use them as well.

Now, before we end this chapter, we need also to take a look at what is known as the Python Shell. The Shell is like an interactive command line driving interface that is found inside of the interpreter that you use. The Shell is important because it will hold onto all of the commands that you decide to write out, and then it will be the part that actually executes that code that you are working with. Any time that you write out a piece of code that is not understandable or that the compiler is not able to work with, the Shell is going to send you an error message, allowing you to know that something is wrong and that you need to go back through and fix it all up.

It is important to be able to add all of these parts to the Python program before you get started with writing in any of the codes that you want. They may sound a bit complicated, and it may seem like a lot of stuff, but without it, you are going to end up with a mess, and the codes are not going to execute the way that you want.

Keep in mind that you are able to go out and get these from a third party source if you would like, but this is often going to add more work and more confusion to the process. As a beginner, if you simply go to the www.python.org part that we talked about before, select the version of Python that you want to go with along with the operating system that is on your computer, you will be able to download the version and it will contain all of the files and the information that you need to get started. This may limit the features that you get to use a bit, but it will make things easier because you won't have to worry about finding the parts later on before writing the code.

There are a lot of different benefits that come with working on the Python language. Whether you have never coded in the past or you are looking to add another language to your set of skills in coding, Python is going to have exactly what you need. And now that you are this far, all the parts that you need in order to write good strong codes will be in place and ready for you to use.

Chapter 2: The Basics of the Python Code

Now that we have the Python code set up on our computers and ready to go, it is time to look at some of the different parts that are needed to write out your codes in Python. There are a lot of different types of codes that you are able to write out, but they are going to all come with the same basic parts. Learning these will help you to get more done with your coding, and will ensure that your codes will work with the compiler. Let's take a look at some of the basic parts that come with the Python code, and how you are able to use these to your own advantage to see the best results.

Learning the keywords

The first part of the Python code that we need to take a look at will be the keywords. There are going to be keywords with any kind of coding language that you are working with, and Python is no different here. These keywords are going to be reserved, and are pretty special because they basically tell your compiler what it needs to do.

These keywords are important because of their one job, which is that they are going to provide the compiler with some commands, and will make sure that the compiler is going to do what you would like. These keywords are going to be important to all of the codes that you decide to do, so make sure that you learn what the keywords are so that you can get the compiler to do what you would like.

Working to name your identifiers

After you have had some time working with the keywords, it is time to look at the identifiers and how we are able to name them. There are actually several types of identifiers that you are able to work, and they will go by names like classes, entities, functions, and variables. Any time that you want to make sure that you are working with an identifier, you will be able to follow the same rules so once you learn it once, you will be all set with this one and able to name all of the identifiers the same way.

So, we need first to take a look at some of the rules that come with naming the identifiers. First, we have to make sure that we carefully choose the names that you choose because you want to make sure that you can remember them later on. There are many different choices that come with the names you can pick, and you can choose from all the letters of the alphabet, including big and small, as well as any numbers you want, the underscore symbol, and any combination of the above that you would like.

There are a few rules to remember that come with this one. First, you can't pick out a name that has a number at the front of it, or there is going to be an error. You also can't add in any spaces show up between the words that you want to write out. this means that you are not able to go with something like 5bears or 5 bears because they are going to show errors from the compiler. But you are able to write out something like fourkids and four_kids to help you name your identifier. Also, you want to make sure that you are not using up any of the keywords to name these.

When it comes to picking out the name that you would like to work with an identifier, make sure that you are able to remember what it is. it can follow all of the rules that we have listed above, but you will find that if you aren't able to remember the name that you gave to it, then it is going to be hard to execute the code and remember what you need to do with it later on. If you spell it in the wrong manner or you call it up under the wrong name, the compiler is not going to know what it is looking for and will send out an error message to you.

With these things in mind, if you pick out a name for the identifier that makes sense with what it is doing, and you make sure that the different rules that we have brought up are followed while naming then you shouldn't have any troubles when it comes to working with naming your identifiers.

Focusing on the control flow

When you work with the idea of any kind of coding language, you will need to pay attention to the control flow. The control flow is going to be there to ensure that the code is written out in the proper manner. There are a few strings in your code that you may want to write out so that the compiler is able to read them the right way. However, if you end up writing out the string in the wrong manner, you will see a few errors on the system. We will take a look at many codes in this guidebook to help you follow the right control flow for this kind of language, which can make it easier to know what you should get done, and how you are able to write out some of the codes with this language.

The idea of the statements

The next thing on the list that we need to take a look at is going to be the statements. You will find that you will work with a lot of statements when you are working with them in Python. These are just the strings of code that you need to write out, and that you would like the compiler to go through and write out on the screen for you.

When you tell the compiler the list of instructions that you want to work with it, you will find that those are the statements of your code. As long as you have been able to write them out properly, the compiler is going to read them and show up the kind of message that you want on the screen. The statements can be as short, or as long, as you would like, depending on the kind of code that you wish to write out.

The comments

The next thing we are going to examine is the comments. There are going to be tied when you are writing out code in Python, and you will want to include an explanation or a note about what you are writing in this code. These notes aren't going to influence how the program works, and you don't want them to even be noticed by your program, but it can help you, and other programmers read the code and know better what is going on in the process.

It is pretty easy to add in these comments the way that you would like this language. You simply need to add the symbol of # ahead of the comment that you are writing. This is going to tell the compiler that you are working on one of these comments and the program, or the compiler is just going to avoid the comment and move on to the next part of the code.

As the coder, you are able to add in as many of these comments to the code as you would like to help explain out the code you are writing, and to keep things flowing nicely. It is actually possible to add one in every other line if you would like, though you want to keep these down a bit to just the ones that are most necessary for your code to work in the proper manner. But as long as you add in that # symbol to the front of the statement, you are able to add in any of these comments, and the compiler will know that you want it to just skip over that part.

Looking at the variables

Another part of the Python code that you need to work with is the variables. These are pretty common with most of the codes that you will write in Python, so it is important to learn them as much as possible The variables are going to be there to store some of the values that you need to keep track of and use in the code, and they can make sure that the different lines of the code are going to be organized and easy to read through.

Adding the value that you want to hit with the variables is going to be easy to do. You just need to place the equal space between the variables and whatever value you would like to assign to them, making sure that the compiler is going to know what it should do there. It is even possible to take this a bit further in order to get a few values to attach with the variables. If you would like, just add in the equal sign between each of them. If you take a look at some of the codes that we work with inside this guidebook, you will notice that there are a lot of variables found in the codes.

The operators

The last basic part of the Python code that we need to take a look at here is the operators. These are going to be another simple option that you are able to work with, but you will notice that they are important that they can be in the codes that you write. You will find that there is actually a wide selection when it comes to working in the operators, and that allows you to really see some differences in how the code works.

For example, you will be able to work with the arithmetic operators to ensure that two parts of the code are going to be added together. You can do the comparison operators to help the programmer compare more than one part of the code together and see if they are the same or not. And you can work with the assigning operators to make sure that the right value is assigned to the right variable.

As we explored a bit with this chapter, there are a lot of different things that come with writing your own code in Python. The basics are meant to be simple so that you are able to really write out the codes that you need without a lot of hard stuff to start you out. There will be a lot more complicated stuff that we can add in later on, but for now, these are some great places to get started.

Chapter 3: Python as an OOP Language

One topic that we need to explore before we get too far into some of the codings with Python that we will do throughout this guidebook is the idea that Python is an object-oriented programming language or an OOP language. If you have looked into the ideas with the Python language in the past, then you may find that this is a term that you have seen in your search, even though you may have no idea what this is going to mean.

To help us understand what this OOP means, and why it is so important to understand how Python works, you will find that any language that is considered OOP is going to be easier to use, especially when it is compared to some of the coding languages that have been around for longer. With languages that are OOP, you see a coding language that wants to classify the classes and objects in a way that is easy to manipulate and work with. We will explore a bit about the classes later in this chapter, which is going to make understanding the OOP language a bit easier.

One feature that is nice to work with when you bring out the idea of an OOP language is that the procedures of any object you use are going to have some power in them to access fields of data, and even to ensure that you can make some modifications to them. With an OOP language, you will be able to design the program in any manner that you want, simply by working with the classes and the objects that are going to go into those classes.

This may seem like a simplistic manner to look at a coding language, and if you have stalled out on learning about a new coding language because you are worried about all of the challenges that are going to come with it, it is easy to feel that something is missing in the process. Or, it is possible that you see this simplicity and feel that the Python coding language, in particular, is not going to have the power that you would like for the programs that you would like to create.

Rest assured, though. You will find that OOP languages, even though they make things a bit easier, are still going to have all of the power that you need. Each language is going to be a bit different in how it is going to use this OOP part, but Python is going to be known as class-based. This means that the code is going to have the objects that you work with fit into a class. This ensures that things stay as organized as possible, and provides easy access to the things that you need when you need them.

You will quickly find that with a bit of practice with the Python code and its OOP functionality, you will be able to write programs with relative ease. If you have ever worked with some of the coding languages in the past, you may notice that some of the older ones are going to not be as organized or as easy to work with as the OOP with Python, and that may have turned you away from programming in the past. But OOP makes it easier and more possible for everyone, whether they are a beginner in coding or not, to do some of the programming's that they want.

Now, when you take a look at some of the features that are found in these OOP languages, you are going to be impressed. These languages are unique in that they are going to, for the most part, rely on the classes to ensure that they work well. In the next section, we will explore a bit more about what these classes are and how they are so powerful, but these ensure that the program is going to work the way that you would like.

Shared features that go with languages that are non-OOP. These languages are going to have some of the same features that are found with low-level features found in the older languages of coding. Some of the features that are still going to be available with the OOP languages like the Python code includes:

The variables: These variables are going to help you out by storing your formatted information inside a few different types of data. These are going to be built into the language and will include things like lists, tables, and strings.

Procedures: These come in with a lot of different names and you may see them called as functions or methods. These procedures are going to be able to take the input that your user provides and then will generate an output that you are able to use to manipulate the data that you have.

Classes and objects: We are soon going to take a bit closer look at the classes and objects, but these are going to be something important when it comes to an OOP language. These classes are going to be kind of like containers that are used to hold and store objects that tend to go with one another. This really adds a level of organization to your code that makes it easier to work with, and easier for the compiler to bring out what you need when you need it.

There are also going to be a few techniques and other structures found in these OOP languages that you need to learn about along the way to help you get some of the results that are needed. However, it is a good idea to look at some of the different features that are likely to show up with this kind of language overall, and are there to ensure that you are able to get the coding that you want to be done in a timely manner. Some of the best features that beginners enjoy when it comes to working with the OOP language include Encapsulation: You will find that when you work with an OOP language, you are going also to have a process that is known as encapsulation to help you. This is the process that has to come into place to bind data together. Any of the functions that are used for this kind of process are important because they are going to manipulate the data and ensure that it is secure from misuse within that code.

Dynamic dispatch and passing of messages. As you work to write some of your codes, you will find that there could be some external codes, but these are not going to be the ones in charge of selecting the procedural code when it is time to execute. This is something that is going to be passed over to the object. The object is going to do this by looking at the method that is associated with that object during run time in a process that is known as dynamic dispatch.

Open recursion: As you work through this OOP language, you may notice that it works with the idea of open recursion. This is basically when the object method is going to find itself called over with another method. You just need to use the keywords of this and self to help the process get going. These are going to be variables called late-bound, which means that they are going to let the method that has been defined in the class at hand invoke a method that you have placed in another class, or that you will define later on.

OOP languages are often a lot easier for coders to work with, especially when they have never been able to do any kind of coding in the past. As you work with a lot of the parts that come with the Python coding language, you will start to see more examples of this OOP feature, and see how it is able to make a big difference in how easy the code is to work with.

The classes and the objects

Now that we have brought up the idea of classes and objects through this chapter, it is time actually to explore these a bit and sees what they are all about. Both of these are going to be critical to making sure that the code will work the way that you want, and that all of the parts of your code show up at the time they are supposed to.

Basically, the classes are going to be the containers that show up in your code. They can be labeled anything that you would like, but often the name is going to have something to do with the objects that you place inside. The objects that are found in the same class need to go together in some manner. They don't have to all be exactly the same, but your goal is to have someone look inside the class and understand why the various objects are inside. With that introduction, let's dive a bit deeper into these classes and objects and see what they are all about and how they work.

Creating your own classes

One thing that is important to learn how to work within the Python coding language is how to create these classes all on your own. The reason that we need to be able to do this is to add in some organization to the code and to make sure that various parts don't end up getting lost along the way. To make one of these classes, you need to be able to learn the keywords that are necessary to name a class.

The neat thing here is that you do get some freedom when you are naming the classes you create. You can give it pretty much any name that you want. But you should have it show up after the chosen keyword, and it works the best if it is given a name that is easy to remember at a later time.

Once you have taken the time to pick out the name that works the best for your class, it is time to name the subclass as well. This subclass is going to be found in the parenthesis of the code, so that makes it easier to find later if you need. Make sure that when this code is written out, and all of the parts have the name that you want to give them that there is a semicolon added to the end. This isn't a necessity, and if you forget it, your code should work just fine. But it is considered the right coding protocol to have it, so make sure to add it in to make things look nicer.

These classes are a simple idea, and it is pretty easy to bring them out and make them work for your needs. But now it is time to learn how to code with them and how to create some of the classes that are the best for your needs. Let's take a quick look at the kind of syntax that you need to work with to make this happen to create a class, and then we can divide the code up into smaller parts to show us how it goes together, and why the code is written the way that it is for creating classes.

```
class Vehicle(object):
#constructor
def_init_(self, steering, wheels, clutch, breaks, gears):
self._steering = steering
self._wheels = wheels
self._clutch = clutch
self._breaks =breaks
self._gears = gears
#destructor
def_del_(self):
    print("This is destructor....")
```

```
#member functions or methods
def Display_Vehicle(self):
    print('Steering:', self._steering)
    print('Wheels:', self._wheels)
    print('Clutch:', self._clutch)
    print('Breaks:', self._breaks)
    print('Gears:', self._gears)
#instantiate a vehicle option
myGenericVehicle = Vehicle('Power Steering', 4, 'Super Clutch',
'Disk Breaks', 5)


myGenericVehicle.Display_Vehicle()
```

Let's take some time to dissect this code to see what is all found inside of it. First, though, open up the compiler and add the code above into it to see what is going to happen. As you write it out, remember some of the different parts of the Python code that we talked about above, and see if you can recognize some of them in the code that we are writing.

Once that code is set up and ready to go, we need to take a look at the class definition that is part of this code. This class definition is going to be the part where you instantiate the object, and then you can add in the definition, so the object ends up going back to the class. This is important to note because it will make sure that the syntax is written into the code in the right manner.

When we are working on the class definition, you want to pay special attention because it is going to be responsible for telling your compiler what has to happen next. If you would like to make sure that you can set up a new definition of the class that you add to the code, the best function to use to make this happen includes object_attribute and object_method to help make it all come together.

Then we can move on and look at the second important part of the code above. We want to make sure that we are writing out the code in a way that is going to give your created class a special attribute. These special attributes will come into play because they give the coder a bit of peace of mind that your objects are going to end up in the right place of the code, and that everything will show up when you run the code, without a big mess.

The code that we wrote out before is going to show us a few examples of how these special attributes work. But there are a few additional special attributes that you may want to pull up and learn how to use as well. Some of the most common special attributes that are used in the Python code will include:

bases: this is considered a tuple that contains any of the superclasses

module: this is where you are going to find the name of the module, and it will also hold your classes.

name: this will hold on to the class name.

doc: this is where you are going to find the reference string inside the document for your class.

dict: this is going to be the variable for the dict. Inside the class name.

With this knowledge about special attributes in place, we also need to take some time to look at the best method to use to access a few of the members, or the objects, that you place into the class that you just created. You want to make sure that your compiler and your text editor are able to recognize the new class that you just created. If these are not able to find or recognize the new class that you were creating, then errors are going to start showing up in this part of the code when you reach it.

We, of course, want to make sure that the compiler is able to read the classes that we are setting up. To make this work, the code has to be set up the right way so that the compiler recognizes that we are creating a new class in the first place. Keep in mind that there are actually a few different methods that you are able to use when it comes to doing this, but the assessor method is often seen as the best one for this and is the easiest of the methods to use. An example of using this assessor method will include:

```
class Cat(object)
        itsAge = None
        itsWeight = None
        itsName = None
        #set accessor function use to assign values to the fields
or member vars
        def setItsAge(self, itsAge):
        self.itsAge = itsAge

        def setItsWeight(self, itsWeight):
        self.itsWeight = itsWeight

        def setItsName(self, itsName):
        self.itsName =itsName
```

```
        #get accessor function use to return the values from a
field
        def getItsAge(self):
        return self.itsAge
        def getItsWeight(self):
        return self.itsWeight

        def getItsName(self):
        return self.itsName


objFrisky = Cat()
objFrisky.setItsAge(5)
objFrisky.setItsWeight(10)
objFrisky.setItsName("Frisky")
print("Cats Name is:", objFrisky.getItsname())
print("Its age is:", objFrisky.getItsAge())
print("Its weight is:", objFrisky.getItsName())
```

The classes that come with the Python coding language are not meant to be that complicated. In fact, they are there to make sure that the Python coding language is a bit easier to work with, especially when it is compared to some of the other coding languages, especially the ones that are a bit older. Learning how to create some of the classes in your code, along with how to place the objects into these new classes, will ensure that you will be able to write some of the best and most powerful codes that you need in the Python language.

Chapter 4: Writing Loops in Python

The next thing that we need to take a look at when it is time to write some of your own codes in Python will be looped. Creating loops can help you to make a code that is more efficient, and will ensure that you are able to get codes written quickly and without a ton of work in the process. These loops work well with some of the conditional statements that we are going to talk about, later on, helping you to clear up your code while getting a lot done in a short amount of time.

Loops are helpful because they are going to speed up how long it is going to take you to write out some codes, can help to clean it all up, and can take hundreds of lines of code (potentially), and put it in just a few lines if needed. Think about how much time that is going to save when you can get all of that code into a few lines with the help of the loops.

If you are working on your code and you find that there are parts of the program that can repeat them over and over again, at least a few times, then the loops are going to help make this happen. You will be able to get the code to repeat as many times as you would like, without having to rewrite the same codes over and over again.

Let's say that you would like to work on some kind of program that has a multiplication table that is going to go from 1 to 10 and all of the answers that are needed for it. Maybe you would choose to do some of the beginner codes and write it all line by line while wasting a ton of time and making it so that the code looks kind of messy in the process. But you are able to use the idea of a lop and write it out with the help of a few lines. We will explore some of the different options that are available for the loops and using them, while also seeing how you would be able to do the example above in just a few lines.

While this may seem like a complex thing to work within the coding, it is actually pretty easy to work with, and even a beginner is going to be able to write out some of these codes. The way that these codes will work is that it tells the compiler to keep reading the same part of the code until there is some condition that is met. Once that condition is met, the compiler will get out of the loop and start working on the next part of the code.

So, let's say that you are working on a program, and a part of it needs to be able to count from one to ten. You would be able to use the idea of the loop in order to tell the compiler to keep going through the code until it reaches higher than ten. We can take a look at a few of the different examples that you are able to do with the ideas of the loop.

One thing to remember here is that when you write out some of these loops, it is important to set up the conditions in the right manner. It is easy to forget to set up these conditions when you first get started, but if you forget them right from the beginning of the code, then you will end up in a loop that is not going to stop. You will get stuck in a continuous loop because the code doesn't know when it needs to stop going through the loop.

When you decide to work with some of the methods that are considered more traditional with coding, or using some of the other methods that are found throughout this guidebook, your whole goal here will be to write out all of the lines of code to get things done. Even if you see some parts of the code repeating, then you would still need to rewrite it out. This could take a long time and may not be as easy to work with as well. But when you work with loops, this is not going to be something that is going to be that big of a deal.

When working with these loops, you are able to get rid of some of the traditional ways of coding and change it up and make things easier. You will be able to combine together a ton of lines of code, or as many as you would need in order to get things done. The compiler will still be able to read through it when the loop is done in the proper way, just as long as you make sure that all of your conditions are put in place.

Now that we have spent some time looking at what the loops mean and why they are going to be so important to your code writing, it is time to divide up some of the different types of loops that are available to help you get this done inside the codes you write.

The first loop: the while loop

So, the first type of loop that we are going to explore is the idea of the while loop in Python. This loop is a good one to bring out and use when you want to make sure that your code is able to go through the loop or the cycle for a predetermined number of times. You can pick out how many times you would like the code to go through this kind of loop to get the best results out of it. This makes it easy to get the number of times you would like the loop to go through.

When you work with the while loop, the goal is not to make the code that you write go through the cycle an indefinite amount of times. But you do have in mind a number of times that you would like the code to do its work. So, if you want to count from one to ten in the code, your goal is to use the while loop in order to go through the loop that many times.

With the while loop, you will see that the code is going to go through the loop, and then it will double check to see if the conditions are met or not. Then, if the conditions are not met, they will go through the loop again and then check again. It will continue doing this over and over again until it has met the conditions, and then it will go on to the other part of the code when the loop is all gone.

To see how the while loop is going to work, and to gain a better understanding of the loop works in general, let's look at some examples of a code that has a while loop inside of it:

```
counter = 1
while(counter <= 3):
        principal = int(input("Enter the principal amount:"))
        numberofyeras = int(input("Enter the number of
years:"))
        rateofinterest = float(input("Enter the rate of
interest:"))
        simpleinterest = principal * numberofyears *
rateofinterest/100
        print("Simple interest = %.2f" %simpleinterest)
        #increase the counter by 1
        counter = counter + 1
```

print("You have calculated simple interest for 3 times!")

Before we take a look at some of the other types of loops that we are able to work with, let's open up the compiler on Python and type in the code to see what is going to happen when we execute it. You will then be able to see how the while loop is able to work. The program is able to go through and figure out the interest rates, along with the final amounts that are associated with it, based on the numbers that the user, or you, will put into the system.

With the example from the code that was above, we have the loop set up so that it is going to go through three times. This means that the user gets a chance to put in different numbers and see the results three times, and then the system will be able to move on. You do get the chance to add in more or take out some loops based on what is the best for your needs.

The second loop: the for loop

At this point, we have been able to take a look at the while loop and what it is all going to entail, it is time to take a look at the for loop so that we are able to see how this in order to do more with loops, and how this is going to be different than the while loop overall. When you work with the while loops, you will notice that the code is going to go through a loop a certain number of times. But it is not always going to work for all of the situations where you want to bring in a loop. And the for loop is going to help us to fill in the blanks that the while loop is not able to do.

When you are ready to work with the for loop, you will be able to set up the code in a manner that the user isn't going to be the one who will go into the code and provide the program with the information that it needs. They do not have the control that is needed to stop the loop from running.

Instead of the user being able to hold the control, the for loop is going to be set up so that it will go over the iteration of your choice in the order that you place the items into your code. This information, when the for loop is going to list them out in the exact way that they are listed in the code. The user will not need to input anything for the for loop to work.

A good example of how this is going to work inside your code so that you are able to make it work for your needs will include the following syntax:

```
# Measure some strings:
words = ['apple,' 'mango,' 'banana,' 'orange']
for w in words:
print(w, len(w))
```

When you work with the for loop example that is above, you are able to add it to your compiler and see what happens when it gets executed. When you do this, the four fruits that come out on your screen will show up in the exact order that you have them written out. If you would like to have them show up in a different order, you can do that, but then you need to go back to your code and rewrite them in the right order, or your chosen order. Once you have then written out in the syntax and they are ready to be executed in the code, you can't make any changes to them.

The third loop: the nested loop

The third and final loop that we are going to work within Python is going to be known as the nested loop. You will find that when we look at the nested loop, there are going to be some parts that are similar to what we looked at with the while loop and with the for loop, but it is going to use these topics in a different way. when you decide to work with a nested loop, you will just take one loop, and then make sure that it is placed inside of another loop. Then, both of these loops will work together and continue on with their work until both have had a chance to finish.

This may seem really hard to work with when it comes to the loops, and you may wonder if there is actually any time that you, as a beginner, would need to work with this loop. But there are often a lot more chances to work with the nested loop than you may think in the beginning. For example, if you are working some kind of code that needs to have a multiplication table inside of it, and you want the answers listed all the way up, then you are going to work with the nested loop.

Imagine how long this kind of process is going to take if you have to go out and list each and every part of the code without using a loop to make it happen. You would have to write out the lines of codes to do one time one, one's times two, and so on until you reach the point where you are at ten times ten. This would end up being a ton of lines of code just to make this kind of table work in your code. But you are able to work with the idea of the nested loop in order to see the results that you want.

A good example that you will be able to work with to show how a nested loop works and to make sure that you are able to make a full multiplication table of your own, includes the following:

#write a multiplication table from 1 to 10
For x in xrange(1, 11):
    For y in xrange(1, 11):
    Print '%d = %d' % (x, y, x*x)

When you got the output of this program, it is going to look similar to this:

1*1 = 1
1*2 = 2
1*3 = 3

1*4 = 4

All the way up to 1*10 = 2

Then it would move on to do the table by twos such as this:

2*1 =2

2*2 = 4

And so on until you end up with 10*10 = 100 as your final spot in the sequence.

Go ahead and put this into the compiler and see what happens. You will simply have four lines of code, and end up with a whole multiplication table that shows up on your program. Think of how many lines of code you would have to write out to get this table the traditional way that you did before? This table only took a few lines to accomplish, which shows how powerful and great the nested loop can be.

As you can see, there are a lot of different things that you are able to do when you start to implement some loops into the codes that you are writing. There are a ton of reasons why you should add a loop into the code you are writing. You will be able to use it in most cases to take a large amount of code and write it in just a few lines instead. This saves you time, cleans up the code that you are trying to light, and the compiler is going to be able to still help you do some things that are super powerful!

Chapter 5: Conditional Statements

```
17      string sInput;
18      int iLength, iN;
19      double dblTemp;
20      bool again = true;

21      while (again) {
22          iN = -1;
23          again = false;
24          getline(cin, sInput);
25          system("cls");
26          stringstream(sInput) >> dblTemp;
27          iLength = sInput.length();
28          if (iLength < 4) {
29              again = true;
30              continue;
31          } else if (sInput[iLength - 3] != '.') {
32              again = true;
33              continue;
34          } while (++iN < iLength) {
35              if (isdigit(sInput[iN])) {
                    continue;
                } else if (iN == (iLength - 3) ) {
```

Another fun topic that we get to spend some time working with when it comes to the Python language is the idea of conditional statements. These are also called the if statements in some cases, or even the decision statements. Learning how to use these will basically teach your computer how to react to the input from the user, even if you are not there to control what is going on.

There are going to be some times in your coding when you will want the program to be able to make some decisions or do some actions on its own, based on what the user tells it, without you needing to go through and code in every piece of the puzzle. Any time that the user is allowed to put in an answer that is all their own, rather than having to pick out from a selection of answers that you provide, then you are working with the decision control statements, or the conditional statements, to make this happen.

There are a few varieties when it comes to working with these kinds of statements, and the one that you go with will be based on what you are trying to do with the code. You can work with the if statement, the if else statement, and the elif statements.

The first option here that we are going to take a look at is known as the if statement. These are going to be pretty simple to work with, and there is not necessarily a lot of power that is behind them. But they will work on the idea that the answer that you get from the user is either seen as true or as false. If it is true, the program will continue on, and if the answer is seen as false, then the program will stop.

You can imagine already that there is going to be a bit of a problem with using the if statement in a lot of cases, and this is why you may not see it all that often. But it is still a good option to start out with when you are learning how these conditional statements are going to work. A good example of how you will be able to use the if statement will be the following:

```
age = int(input("Enter your age:"))
if (age <=18):
        print("You are not eligible for voting, try next election!")
print("Program ends")
```

Let's explore what is going to happen with this code when you put it into your program. If the user comes to the program and puts that they are younger than 18, then there will be a message that shows up on the screen. In this case, the message is going to say "You are not eligible for voting, try next election!" Then the program, as it is, is going to end. But what will happen to this code if the user puts in some age that is 18 or above?

With the if statement, nothing will happen if the user says that their age is above 18. The if statement just has one option and will focus on whether the answer that the user provides is going to match up with the conditions that you set with your code. The user has to put in that they are under the age of 18 with the if statement in this situation, or you won't be able to get the program to happen again.

As we mentioned a bit before, there are going to be times when the if statement could cause some problems. You naturally want the user to put in their actual age when they join the program, rather than only putting in the right answers. And if nothing shows up in your program when the user puts in the wrong age, this is going to leave them with something that makes no sense, or even a program that ends. It's likely that this is not what you want to work with.

This is where the if else statements are going to start showing up, and you will quickly find that they are more useful to work with than the plain if statements. The if else statements are going to work with the idea that we just did and then takes it a step further. The point with the if else statement is to make sure that the program does something, no matter what answer they are able to give to the program.

Going with the idea of the example that we talked about above, you may want to go through and separate the people out into two groups. You may have a group who is 18 and under, and a group that is over 18 years old. This is something that the if else statement is going to be able to help you work with, and will ensure that, no matter what answer the user adds in for their age, something comes up. A good example of the code that you are able to use when it is time to bring in the if else statements include:

```
age = int(input("Enter your age:"))
if (age <=18):
        print("You are not eligible for voting, try next election!")
else
        print("Congratulations! You are eligible to vote. Check out your local polling station to find out more information!)
print("Program ends")
```

As you can see, this really helps to add some more options to your code and will ensure that you get an answer no matter what results the user gives to you. You can also change up the message to say anything that you want, but the same idea will be used no matter the answer that the user gives.

The example above is going to be a pretty simple one to work with. You can add in as many possibilities to the if else statements as you would like and you do not have to limit yourself to just two options as we did above. If you only need to work with two options, then this is fine to stick with. But there are lots of codes that need to expand to more, and the if else statement is going to help with that as well.

For example, maybe you want to split the individuals who come to your program into five different age groups rather than just the two from before. You can just go through and add in an if part of the statement, along with a message that you would like to go with it and continue on with the if else statements. You can technically add in as many options as you would like based on the kind of code that you are trying to develop.

Another example of using the if else statement is when you are creating a program that wants the person to pick out their favorite type of drink. There are a lot of options out there when it comes to tasty drinks, and you can definitely expand out the if else statements. Maybe you pick out a few options like pop, milk, juice, and coffee. Then you can add in the else statement that is going to be your "catch-all" in case the user decides to pick water or something else as their favorite drink. When this is in place, no matter what answer the user gives to the program there will be some kind of result that shows up.

Adding a catch-all to the end of your code, or the "else" part of this, can be important. You can't always think about all the different examples that the person may put in. You could put a hundred options into your code (which would take a lot of time and be messy and not really necessary), and then the user will name a color differently or pick the one color that you forgot. If you don't have that as an option, then the program won't know how to behave from there.

The else statement here is important because it helps you to catch all of the remaining answers that the user could give you. If you don't have a statement in the code to handle the answer that the user gives, then the else statement will make sure to get you covered. Just make sure that you have that else statement in place to get it done.

The elif statements

We have spent some time talking about two of the conditional statements that are available for Python coding. The first ones, the if statements are a good place to start to get some practice with the conditional statements. They are based on the idea of the answer the user giving you is true or false. If the user gives an answer that is seen as true, then the program will finish up what you have next in the code. If the answer is seen as something false, then the program is going to end. It is meant to be something that is simple to work with and can give you some practice with writing codes.

Then you can move on to the if else statements if your code needs something a bit more to it. With the if else statements, we took this a bit further and set up something that is going to make sure that the user is going to get some kind of results, no matter what answer they put into the system. We even looked at a few examples of how you would be able to use the if else statement so we can see how they are different compared to the if statements.

And the third type of conditional statement that you can work with when you want to code in Python is known as the elif statement. The elif statement is going to be great to work with because it allows the user to look at a few options that you can present them with, and then, based on the kind of answer that the user gives, the program is going to execute the results that you added into the code for it.

You will actually see a lot of different programs that are going to rely on the elif statements. One place where you may see this kind of conditional statement is when you play a game, and there is a menu that starts up on the program then this is a good sign that an elif statement is being used. These conditional statements are going to be useful when it comes to providing a few options to the user, rather than one or two.

When you use the elif statements, you get a bit of freedom with what you are going to add into the code. You can choose to add in just a few options, or you can add in quite a bit, as long as you write this code out in the right way and you double check that the right function is put in the right place. In addition, you may want to keep the number of these that you use to a minimum because having too many is going to add some complexity to the code. You have to decide if this is what you would like to do.

One of the best ways to determine how to use the elif statements and whether it is going to work in the code that you are trying to write is to look at some examples of how the elif statement works. The following syntax can be used to write an elif statement:

if expression1:
statement(s)
elif expression2:
statement(s)
elif expression3:
statement(s)
else:
statement(s)

This is a pretty basic syntax of the elif statement and you can add in as many of these statements as you would like. Just take that syntax and then place the right information into each part and the answer that is listed next to it. Notice that there is also an else statement at the end of this. Don't forget to add this to your code so that it can catch any answer that the user puts in that isn't listed in your elif statements.

To help you better understand how these elif statements work and how the syntax above is going to work, let's take a look at a little game that you can create using these statements:

Print("Let's enjoy a Pizza! Ok, let's go inside Pizzahut!")
print("Waiter, Please select Pizza of your choice from the menu")
pizzachoice = int(input("Please enter your choice of Pizza:"))
if pizzachoice == 1:
        print('I want to enjoy a pizza napoletana')
elif pizzachoice == 2:
        print('I want to enjoy a pizza rustica')
elif pizzachoice == 3:
        print('I want to enjoy a pizza capricciosa')
else:
        print("Sorry, I do not want any of the listed pizza's, please bring a Coca Cola for me.")

When you add this into your code, the user is going to have the benefit of going through this part of the program and making the choice based on what they want. And if you get it set up the proper way, you will have the right answer come up for them. So, if the user decides that they would like to choose the pizza rustica, they would need to go through and select number 2. If they want to have just a drink and none of the pizza options that are listed, then they would click on that.

Remember you are able to add in as many options as you would like to the conditional statements of the elif statement. It is all about what works the best for your program. You may have four options, or you can have twenty, but try to keep these to just the ones that your program needs to function in the proper manner for your needs.

As you can see here, the conditional statements are going to work well to help you gain more power in your codes, and they will help you to get the program to work, even if you are not able to guess all of the answers that someone is going to give you in the program. It allows the program to make some of the decisions without you while ensuring that your code is going to behave while the user is interacting with it. Make sure to try out some of the examples of conditional statements in the compiler to see how these work and to get more familiar with the way that you are able to use these.

Chapter 6: Raising an Exception

We have spent some time looking at some of the different things that you are able to work on when you bring out the Python code. Now it is time to bring up a new idea of what you are able to do, which is to raise exceptions. We need to focus on how to raise some of your own exceptions in the codes that you write, as well as how to handle any exceptions that the computer program decides to raise on its own.

The more that you work with coding in Python, you will find that the program is going to bring out some of its own exceptions as you go. There are a few exceptions that are part of the Python code, so it is able to behave in the manner that you want it too. But then there is also a chance when you will purposely add into the program so that it raises an exception and behaves the way that you would like.

The ones that the program is going to raise on its own will be automatic because they are already placed into the Python library. A good example of this one is when the user tries to divide by zero in the code. The Python library is set up not to let this happen so it will raise the exception for you. On the other hand though, if there is a new exception that you would like to work with that is just for your own program that you are working on. You can rise up an exception to work with any kind of program that you want.

As the programmer here, you will want to learn how to work with all of the exceptions that are found within the Python library. When you know how these exceptions work, it is easier to add what you need into the code, and you can even learn when the exceptions will start to turn up for you. While there are a lot of exceptions that are out there, some of the most common exceptions and the keywords that come with the Python code include:

Finally—this is the action that you will want to use to perform cleanup actions, whether the exceptions occur or not.

Assert—this condition is going to trigger the exception inside of the code

Raise—the raise command is going to trigger an exception manually inside of the code.

Try/except—this is when you want to try out a block of code and then it is recovered thanks to the exceptions that either you or the Python code raised.

How to raise an exception in your code

The first thing that we need to take a look at when we learn about exceptions inside of code is how we can use them. When those automatic exceptions start to show up, it is important to be prepared and learn how you can take some steps to make the exceptions make more sense.

So, when you work on your code, and you see that there is an issue or an exception that starts to show up, or you want to figure out why it seems that your program is doing something that seems off, you can look and see whether or not your compiler is raising a new exception. These are going to be raised when the code is looking through your work and can't figure out what steps it should take next to make the program work the way that you want.

The good news is that many times, the issues that come up with these exceptions are going to be simple and easy to fix. For example, it could be something as simple as trying to call up a file, but you misspelled a word or called it the wrong thing, either when you are calling it up or when you saved it. The compiler won't be able to find the file because it is not all matching up, but you can just go back in and fix that problem in a few seconds and get the best results.

Let's take a look at how you are able to make these exceptions work. The best way to understand how exceptions are going to work and make sure we understand what it is going to look like when the compiler decides to raise an exception is to do an example of our own. The following is a simple exception that we can use to study for this endeavor:

$x = 10$

$y = 10$

result = x/y #trying to divide by zero

print(result)

The output that you are going to get when you try to get the interpreter to go through this code would be:

>>>

Traceback (most recent call last):

    File "D: \Python34\tt.py", line 3, in <module>

    result = x/y

ZeroDivisionError: division by zero

>>>

Taking a look at the example that is above, you will see that the compiler will try to read through it and will bring up an error for you. The only reason that this happens is that you or the user is trying to divide by zero at some point. You have a few options from this point. You can either leave things the way that they are and run the program in the manner that it is now, which provides you with an error message that is kind of messy and hard to read. Or you can make some changes to determine exactly what that message should be saying to the user.

For most programmers, it is agreed that you should try to change up the error message at least a bit. This helps to eliminate the messy message that no one really understands, and makes it easier for the user to understand why they are getting the error message in the first place. When the exception is raised, you do not want the user to be confused as to what they should do next, or they may get frustrated and not want to use the program any longer. Raising an exception and making sure that you have it organized the right way will make your user enjoy the program that much more. A good example of how to clean up the exceptions a bit will include the following:

```
x = 10
y = 0
result = 0
try:
        result = x/y
        print(result)
except ZeroDivisionError:
        print("You are trying to divide by zero.")
```

As you can see, the code that we just put into the compiler is going to be pretty similar to the one that we wrote above.

But we did go through and change up the message to show something there when the user raises this exception. When they do get this exception, they will see the message "You are trying to divide by zero" come up on the screen. This isn't a necessary step, but it definitely makes your code easier to use!

How to define your own exceptions

With the examples that we did above, we were focusing on how we could raise an exception based on what is seen as an error or an issue with the Python library. But now we need to take this a bit further and see what else we can do. You will be able to use Python in order to create some of your own codes along the way, which design your own programs as well. And there may be times when you want to change up the rules and have an exception raised based on what is allowed and what is not allowed for your program.

These exceptions are not going to be ones found in the Python library. And that is just fine. But because of this, you need to be able to write out the code in a manner that allows it to bring up that exception because the Python library is not going to do it for you at all.

For example, you may be working on your own program, and you decide that when your user is on it, they should only be able to add in certain numbers to the code, and the others are going to be wrong. This may work best when you decide to create a program or a game to play. Or you could have it so that an exception comes up if you only want the user to have a chance to answer the question three times rather than them doing it an indefinite number of times. If they get it right, then the program would go on. If they get it wrong, then the exception will be raised after the third time.

These kinds of exceptions may not be found in the Python library, but they are going to be important to how well the program can work and the results that you will be able to get from them. And they can ensure that the program you are writing, no matter what kind of program it is, will work in the proper manner. A good example of the code that you can write out to make this happen will include:

```
class CustomException(Exception):
def_init_(self, value):
```

```
        self.parameter = value
def_str_(self):
        return repr(self.parameter)


try:
        raise CustomException("This is a CustomError!")
except CustomException as ex:
        print("Caught:", ex.parameter)
```

When you finish this particular code, you are done successfully adding in your own exception. When someone does raise this exception, the message "Caught: This is a CustomError!" will come up on the screen. You can always change the message to show whatever you would like, but this was there as a placeholder to show what we are doing. Take a moment here to add this to the compiler and see what happens.

In the beginning, it may seem like exception handling is going to be a bit silly and like it is not worth your time to learn how to use this at all. You may assume that only certain kinds of programs are going to work well with these exceptions and that anything else is just a waste of time to learn this.

However, you may be surprised at how often you would need to bring these exceptions up for your needs. Even in programs that are not too complex, or in programs that don't really need the exception to be raised in the first place, there can be some benefit to using them, and learning how to change up the message, as well as raise some of your own along the way. it is definitely something that you should learn how to do well when you decide to write your own codes in the Python language.

As you start to work on your codes more and try to make them a bit more advanced in Python, you will notice that raising exceptions is something that will become pretty common to you. There are a lot of times that you can work with exceptions, whether you are working on some that are unique to your own program, or some that are recognized by the Python library on its own.

Working with some of the codes and examples that we explored in this chapter will ensure that you are well on your way to seeing some great success with exceptions and that you will be able to make these work well for your needs. It may take a bit of time to learn, but adding these to your compiler, and getting some practice, can be a great way to help you out!

Chapter 7: The Beauty of Inheritances in the Python Language

There are a lot of different things that you are able to work on when you decide to add Python into the mix. You will be able to write some awesome codes along the way, and even as a beginner you are going to find that you can write codes to do anything that you would like. But now we are going to focus a bit on how you can write out inheritances in Python and why it is such an important part of the Python code.

Inheritances are a nice addition to your skills with Python because they will ensure that you can write out some complex parts of the code, without having to rewrite it a bunch of times. This helps to not only clean up the code and make it look nicer but can also make writing out the code a bit easier overall as well. It allows you to reuse a specific part of the code that you need, without having to rewrite it.

To help make the idea of how inheritances work a bit easier to understand, you have to remember that this type of coding is going to take an original code, one that you already wrote out earlier, and copy it down to make up a new part of the code that is based on the first one. The first part of this is going to be called the parent code, and the second part is going to be the child code.

The child code can be changed around and adjusted in any manner that you want, and there will be no changes to the parent code when you do this. This allows you a bit more freedom with what you are working on and ensures that this is going to behave the way that you want. You can also make as many of these children codes as you would like based on what needs to happen to make your code work properly.

While this may, at first, sound a bit complicated, inheritances are pretty easy to learn. You will have to go through a few steps to make it happen, and it may look like a lot of code, but it ends up being a lot less than what you would see if you just rewrote the code rather than using the inheritance all of the time. A good example of how these inheritances can work will include the following:

```
#Example of inheritance
#base class
class Student(object):
        def init_(self, name, rollno):
        self.name = name
        self.rollno = rollno
#Graduate class inherits or derived from Student class
class GraduateStudent(Student):
        def init_(self, name, rollno, graduate):
        Student_init_(self, name, rollno)
        self.graduate = graduate

def DisplayGraduateStudent(self):
        print"Student Name:", self.name)
        print("Student Rollno:", self.rollno)
        print("Study Group:", self.graduate)
```

```
#Post Graduate class inherits from Student class
class PostGraduate(Student):
        def_init_(self, name, rollno, postgrad):
        Student_init_(self, name, rollno)
        self.postgrad = postgrad

        def DisplayPostGraduateStudent(self):
        print("Student Name:", self.name)
        print("Student Rollno:", self.rollno)
        print("Study Group:", self.postgrad)

#instantiate from Graduate and PostGraduate classes
        objGradStudent = GraduateStudent("Mainu", 1, "MS-
Mathematics")
        objPostGradStudent = PostGraduate("Shainu", 2, "MS-
CS")
        objPostGradStudent.DisplayPostGraduateStudent()
```

When you type this into your interpreter, you are going to get the results:

('Student Name:', 'Mainu')
('Student Rollno:', 1)
('Student Group:', 'MSC-Mathematics')

('Student Name:', 'Shainu')

('Student Rollno:', 2)

('Student Group:', 'MSC-CS')

As a coder, you will find that these inheritances are going to help you gain some freedom when you write out the codes. If you are able to take a parent class or the base class, and you want to make sure that it works later on with your child or derived class, the inheritance is going to ensure that you are able to do this while keeping the features of the parent class that you want, and kicking out the features that won't work for you. Add in that you can also add in some new things if needed to the child class, and you can see why the inheritances are going to be a great option for you.

As you work with the inheritances, remember that you have the freedom to add in as many of the derived classes as you want from the original base class. As long as you make sure that they are done in the order that you need them to, such as what we did with the example above, you will be able to have as many of these derived classes as are needed to get the work done. And you can even change up each level of this to end up with the results that you want along the way.

How to override my base class

The next thing that we need to take a look at when we look at inheritances is the idea of overriding one of the base classes that you have. There are going to be times when you have a class that is derived, and you would like to take the right steps that are needed to override things that are found in the base class. This means that you will see the base class and then change up some of the behavior that is inside of it. This is going to ensure that you are able to create a base class that has the behavior that you want from the derived class, along with some other behaviors that are needed in your code.

It may sound like this is going to add in too much complexity to the process, but it is a great way to give you the power to control which parental features you would like to have shown up in your derived class when you create it. This will be the easiest way for you to make sure that the right features end up in your new class while maintaining some of the parental features that you want as well in that class.

Trying out some overloading

In addition to being able to override the base class and get some of the other options sorted out and ready to go, you can also use a process with your inheritances that are known as overloading. When you decide to work with overloading, you will take one of the identifiers and use it to help define two or more methods at a time. For most cases, there are going to be no more than two methods in the class, but sometimes this number can go a bit higher.

The two methods that you want to use with overloading need to be found in the same class. They will have parameters that are different, so make sure they come with different processes. Overloading will then work for you when you have them do a task that has to be done under the different parameters.

Overloading is a bit more complex to work with than what most beginners will need. But as you explore more of what can be done with the Python language over time, and you work on more codes, you are sure to run across times when it is needed.

A final note concerning inheritances

As you are working on a variety of codes in Python, you may come across times when one inheritance is not enough, and you will want to write out several at a time. This process is known as multiple inheritances, and when you do this, you will find that each level is going to have some similarities to one another, but each level can still allow for some smaller changes. You can just keep going doing the line, repeating the steps that you did in the example before.

When you start to do some codes that need multiple inheritances, you will take one class, also known as your base class, and you will give it at least two parent classes to get started. This is an important thing to learn when you are growing your code because you can really help to use it to get the code written out as long as you need.

Multiple inheritances can be as simple or as complicated as you would like to make them. When you work on them, you will be able to create a brand new class, which we will call Class C, and you got the information to create this new class from the previous one, or Class B. Then you can go back and find that Class B was the one that you created from information out of Class A. Each of these layers is going to contain some features that you like from the class ahead of it, and you can go as far into it as you would like. Depending on the code that you decide to write, you could have ten or more of these classes, each level having features from the previous one to keep it going.

When you decide to create one of the multiple inheritances, remember that while you can keep going down the line and making as many derived classes as you would like, the circular inheritance is not allowed. You can add in as much of the parent class that the derived classes need to code, but you can't go around and make a circle connect things with this kind of method.

As you get more into the Python code and you write some of your own codes in the process, you will find that working with all of these inheritances can be popular because they help to keep the code organized and neat. There are a lot of times when you are able to reuse the same block of code throughout the program, with just a few changes, while saving your time and your fingers from rewriting all of those codes again.

Chapter 8: The Regular Expressions

The next type of coding skill that we are going to take a look at is known as a regular expression. When you work with the Python coding language, one thing that you will notice is the library that comes with it. This library is going to contain a lot of different options including regular expressions, which can help you handle all of your searches while making sure that the right actions happen behind the scenes as well.

These expressions are important because they help the compiler help you filter out different texts or strings of texts.

It is possible for you to use this in order to check and see if a text or some string of text is found in the code you are working with and then match it back up to the regular expression as you see fit. When you are ready to write out some of your regular expressions it is possible to stick with a syntax that is similar each time, no matter what option you are using. It even works in other languages so even if you go from Python to another coding language, you will use the same syntax.

Now, you may be reading through this and have some questions about what regular expressions really are and how you would be able to use them to get things to work out well with your codes. A good place for us to start with this is to bring out our text editor and have the program try to locate a word, one that was spelled out in different manners in the same code. We will take a look at a few ways that you can do this with regular expressions so that this makes a bit more sense as you go through.

You will find that there are a lot of times when you will be able to use regular expressions when writing Python codes. This is why it is so important for us to figure out how to write them. The first step to consider when you want to work with the regular expressions is to import the expression library. This often happens when you first start up your Python program to see if it did that for you or not. You should get in the habit of doing this though because you will use it on a regular basis.

When it is time to work on writing some statements in Python, you will often need to bring up some regular expressions. As soon as you know all that the regular expressions are able to help you to do, you will see a lot of power show up in some of the codes that you write. Let's explore a bit about how the regular expressions work, how they can be used in your codes, and how you are able to work to make them perform the way that you want in the code.

Looking at the basic patterns with regular expressions

The first thing that we have to explore when we are working with regular expressions is that they are available to use in a lot of different kinds of equations and characters, rather than just one kind. This is going to make it easier for you to watch for some of the patterns that are going to show up when you need them. As you work with regular expressions, you will start to see that there are a few patterns that are pretty common and will show up often with these and they include:

a, X, 9, < -- ordinary characters just match themselves exactly. The meta-characters that aren't going to match themselves simply because they have a special meaning include: . ^ $ * ? { [] and more.

. (the period)—this is going to match any single except the new line symbol of '\n'

3. \w—this is the lowercase w that is going to match the "word" character. This can be a letter, a digit, or an underbar. Keep in mind that this is the mnemonic and that it is going to match a single word character rather than the whole word.

\b—this is the boundary between a non-word and a word.

\s—this is going to match a single white space character including the form, form, tab, return, newline, and even space. If you do \S, you are talking about any character that is not a white space.

^ = start, $ = end—these are going to match to the end or the start of your string.

\t, \n, \r—these are going to stand for tab, newline, and return

\d—this is the decimal digit for all numbers between 0 and 9. Some of the older regex utilities will not support this so be careful when using it

\ --this is going to inhibit how special the character is. If you use this if you are uncertain about whether the character has some special meaning or not to ensure that it is treated just like another character.

Of course, these are not the limits of the regular expression that you can add into your code, but they are some of the most common ones that you are going to rely on as a beginner. There are a lot of different codes where you are going to need them, and it is possible that you will want to bring in more than one regular expression in the mix.

Doing a query with your regular expressions

In addition to doing some of the work as we did above to find the basic patterns in your Python code, it is possible to bring out the regular expressions to help you to do a search on any of the input strings in the code. The neat thing with this one is that there are going to be several methods that you can use for this, based on what you are looking for in the code.

Every time that you are ready to do a query, you may find that you need to do something a bit different based on what you want to get out of the process. Working with regular expressions on the Python code will make sure that you are able to pick out the right queries to get things done. Let's look at three of the most common query results that you are able to use when working on a Python code.

The search method

The first of the three query methods that we are going to work with is known as the search() method. This is a good one to rely on because it will let you match up a text or a string of text to another one, no matter where it ends up in the code. This function isn't going to come with a lot of restrictions like you may see with the other two. It is going to work the best when you want to be able to search through the whole string of text for the answer, rather than just the end of the string.

This means that the search method is going to be able to look inside a string of text and find whether something is there or not, no matter where this match is going to show up. A good example of how you can use the search method includes:

```
import re
string = 'apple, orange, mango, orange'
match = re.search(r'orange', string)
print(match.group(0))
```

Take a moment to add this to your compiler and see what output you get. This code is going to give you an output of "orange". With this method, you are only going to see the match one time. There could be ten oranges in the code, the search function will just tell you if one is there, not how many of that item are in the string. Even though there are technically two oranges in the code above, the search() method will just return one of them to you. Once it finds that first orange, it has done its job and will stop. Later we will discuss another method that you can use that can help you know exactly how many of an item are in the string.

The match method

There are a lot of times when you will be able to bring out the search method and make it work in your code, but there are also other types of queries that you will want to work with. And the second type of query that we are going to look at is the match method. This one is going to find the matches again, but it will only check to see if the match is found at the beginning of your string, rather than anywhere in the string. It is the best query to work with for looking for a specific pattern inside the syntax that you are searching for.

We can see how the match method is going to be different by comparing it to the search method from before. You can see that there is a pattern, where the object "orange' is going to show up alternating with the other words there. but when you work with the match function, you would switch out the research with the re_match instead. In this case, based on how the pattern is right now, you are not going to get any results because the word orange is not the first one in the string of text.

Even though you can see that orange is in the code, it is not going to be the first part of the string. In what we have written out, Apple is going to be the first word in this string.

The match method is just looking to see if there is a match between the first word or not, and since orange is not going to be that first word, it is not going to show up.

You can always change around the order of the words that are found inside of the code, you will be able to really get it to work out the way that you want. But the match method is only going to compare the search term with the first term that is in your string of text.

The findall method

And the third query option that we can work with when it comes to the regular expressions will be the findall method. With the other two methods, you will just find out whether the object you are trying to match will show up in the string, either anywhere in the string or at the beginning of the string. But the findall method is going to be a bit different. This one tells you how many times the object is going to show up inside your string of text in the first place. So, if we use the option from before, you will use the findall method and get the result of "orange, orange". Since there is two present, this is going to give you two options to work with.

You are going to have some options here because there can be as many of the same object in the string as needed, or you can pick out another kind of object as well. If you added twenty oranges into this, the findall method would list out orange twenty times when you used it. Or, if you change this and try to look up apple you would only get one apple back as a result here.

Try out the final method and find out how it is different compared to the search and the match method that we worked with. You can just type in the code from the compiler that we had before and change out the method that you are working with. Add some things, take some things away, and then see how these three are going to work with each other. This is the best way to get used to working with the query options when it comes to regular expressions.

Chapter 9: What is Scikit-Learn and Other Libraries That Work Well with Python?

Now that we have had some time to look through the Python code and some of the different things that we are able to do with this code. There are a number of libraries that you are able to work with when it comes to Python, which is going to make it even easier to do some of the different codes that you would like to work with.

You can easily just work with the regular kind of library that comes with Python, which gives you a lot of freedom and you will be able to use them in order to handle the codes that we have been looking at in this guidebook. But there are times when you will want to work with a different kind of library based on what is going to happen with the code you are writing. For example, if you want to work with machine learning, the Scikit-Learn library is going to be a good option to look at.

There are a lot of different libraries that you are able to work with based on what you want to do with your coding. But the main libraries that we are going to look at will include Numpy, Matplotlib, Scipy, and Scikit-Learn.

NumPy

The first Python library that we are going to take a look at is NumPy. This is a good library to work with that helps to add in some more support as needed for large and multi-dimensional arrays and matrices. It is also going to include a bigger collection of high-level mathematical functions so that you can actually use your codes to operate these arrays. The original ancestor library that came before this one, known as Numeric, was created by Jim Hugunin, and then was changed over to NumPy by Travis Oliphant. Over the years, more contributors are going to help develop the NumPy over the years, and it is open sourced which will allow us to really see what can work with it over time.

The Python programming language was able to do a lot of different things over time. With that said, in the beginning, it wasn't designed to do any computing of numbers. However, because it is so easy to work with and has enough power that goes with it, it was able to attract the attention of the scientific and engineering community early on, and this group was interested in learning how they could use Python for their own needs.

Because of this, in 1995 a special interest group, which went under the name of matrix-sig, was founded and their aim was to make a computing package that can work with arrays and handle some of the numerical computing that scientists and engineers could use. Among the members of this group was the well-known Python maintainer and designer named Guido van Rossum, who then implemented some of these extensions of the Python syntax (in particular, it is going to use the indexing syntax, to make the array computing a bit easier overall.

One of the goals that came with this is that it was meant to replace Numerically, and hopefully, it would come in as being a bit more flexible compared to the older version. Like Numeric, it is now deprecated. Numarray, a version of NumPy, had a faster operation for some of the larger arrays, but on some of the smaller ones, it would be slower.

Numeric and Numarray were in competition for some time, but then in 2005, the developer known as Travis Oliphant wanted to be able to make both of these, and take the benefits of each and turn them into one program or one library that would work the best for everyone. The new project became a part of the larger SciPy programming methods that were going on at the same time. However, to make sure that programmers were not needing to install the large SciPy package in order to get the NumPy program out of it, this was separated out. You can choose to either just get the SciPy library if you feel like you need more than one library from it, but if you are just interested in working with NumPy, you will be able to do this on its own as well.

So, to make this a bit easier to look at, let's explore a bit about what the NumPy library is all about, and why this is going to be such an important library to work with. Some of the things that make up the NumPy library to help us see why it is so important to include:

NumPy is going to be a numerical library available through Python that is open source so anyone is able to use it and see how it will work for them.

You will find that this library is going to contain a multi-dimensional matrix and array data structure.

You will be able to do quite a few operations that are mathematical on arrays. Some of the options that you are able to use with this one will include transformation, algebraic, and mathematical functions.

It is possible to work with random number generators as well.

NumPy is known as a wrapper that is going to be a library that can be implemented in C.

Pandas objects will rely on the objects of NumPy. Basically, these Pandas are going to extend the NumPy.

If you plan to work with the NumPy library, then this is a sign that you want to be able to write some of your own mathematical equations with the library. This makes it easier for you to really do some of the algebraic equations and other mathematical things that are a bit harder to work with if you just use the regular Python library. Not everyone is going to want to work with this option, but for some programmers it is necessary. The good news with this one is that you will be able to download just the NumPy library if you choose, making it easier to work with this library, without a lot of bloat and other objects and features that you do not need.

Matplotlib

Another kind of library that you may choose to work with is going to be the Matplotlib. This one is a bit different than the library that we talked about before, and you will have to determine if this is a library that you will want to use along with the NumPy library from above, or if you will want to use this on its own. Not all programs are going to need this library, but it is still a good one to know about because, depending on the kinds of programs that you decide to write, you may need to bring this into the mix at some point.

Matplotlib is going to be one of the plotting libraries for the Python programming language. The neat thing is that this is a kind of extension that comes with NumPy, so if you do use that previous library, it is likely that you will need to bring in the Matplotlib as well. This extension is going to help you do some more numerical mathematics as well, but it is going to focus a bit more about the graphs and charts that you will want to work with that are based on the numbers that you have.

Matplotlib is going to be able to provide your program with an object-oriented API to embed plots into the application with a variety of different toolkits based on what you would like to use. This one is going to resemble the MATLAB that you may have heard about in the past, though the use of this is going to be highly discouraged. If you plan to use SciPy, which we will talk about in a bit, you will need to use the Matplotlib as well.

To take a look at the history of this library, you will find that John D. Hunter was the original writer of this library and it currently has a very active development community. This is good news if you plan to use the library because it means that the library is going to be developed and used a lot in the future and that any updates are going to be made available to you as quickly as possible.

Since this is an open-sourced library that you are able to work with, it has been changed up in order to support a lot of different versions of Python that are popular today. As of the summer of 2017, this library is able to support Python 2.7 to Python 3.6. However, since so many people are working with Python 3 right now, it is believed that by 2020, the library is not going to be supported on Python 2 any longer.

To help us get a better understanding of this kind of library, we also need to take some time to compare the Matplotlib to the idea of MATLAB. Pyplot is going to be a module that is found in Matplotlib and it is going to provide the computer with a MATLAB-like interface. Matplotlib is going to be designed in a manner that you are able to use it with MATLAB if you would like, and this allows you to use Python. The main advantage is that this makes it free and open source. You can choose whether you want to work with this or not with your own coding.

As we mentioned a bit before, you will be able to use the Matplotlib in order to deal with graphics and charts when you are working with the Python language. You are able to use it for a lot of different things including Python scrips, the shell, web application servers, and some other graphical user interface toolkits based on what you would like to do.

The neat thing here is that you can work with a lot of different tools in order to extend out the functionality of matplotlib. Different companies and developers have worked with these, and they are often going to be separate downloads. There are a few that can be downloaded at the same time as the source code for matplotlib, but they may have some external dependencies. Some of the ones that you may want to consider working with will include:

Basemap: This is going to be a toolkit that can help you to plot maps. This can include things like political boundaries, coastlines, and map projections.
Cartopy: This is going to be a mapping library that is going to include a lot of different options including image transformation capabilities, line, and polygon capabilities to name a few.

Excel tools: This is going to be a library that is able to provide you with some utilities to exchange the data you have with Microsoft Excel.

Mplot3d: This is the part that you are going to want to use with any 3D plots you want to do.

Natgrid: This is going to be an interface to the natgrid library for irregular gridding of the spaced data.

There are a few different types of plots and graphs that you are going to be able to use when you download and use the library of Matplotlib from Python. Some of the different types of graphs and plots that you are able to work with when you are doing this kind of library include:

The bar graph: A bar graph is going to rely on bars to help us compare data that shows up between different categories. It is going to be a good option if you would like to take a look at the changes that occur over a period of time. and you are able to represent it going either vertically or horizontally. In addition, this one works in a manner that shows us that the longer the bar is, the greater the value associated with it.

The histogram: Histograms are going to be used to help us see the distribution of something. These are going to be the most helpful when we are looking at a list that is really long or we work with arrays.

Scatterplot: Another option that you can go with is known as the scatter plot. The scatter plot is going to be used when you would like to compare variables, especially when you want to know how much one variable is going to be affected by another variable in order to build up a relationship that shows up there. The data for the scatter plot is going to be displayed as a collection of points, and the value that you have for one of your variables will determine the position on the horizontal axis. Then the value of the other variable is going to tell us the position that shows up on the vertical axis as well.

Area plot: This one is going to be similar to a line plot, and you may hear them called as a stack plot. These plots are meant to help the programmer track changes that occur over time for two or more related groups that will make up one whole category.

Pie chart: There may be some times when you want to work with a pie chart, and this library will help you to get it done. The pie chart is going to be a circular graph that can be broken down into smaller segments based on the information that you have. it is going to look similar to a pie, and each slice is going to show us the categories that you are working with at the time.

These are just a few of the different graphs and charts that you will be able to work with when it comes to the matplotlib library. It is going to be an extension that comes with the NumPy library that we talked about before, and you may find that these are both going to work together well. In fact, once you are done doing some of the mathematical equations from before, you will be able to take that information and turn it into some of the charts that are found with matplotlib.

If you are planning on doing some work with numbers and charts, you will find that the regular library that comes with Python is just not going to be able to do all of the work on its own. This just wasn't what it was designed to do in the first place. But if this is something that is important to you and you need to get that done with the help of Python, then adding in the NumPy and the Matplotlib libraries are the best options to make this happen.

SciPy

The last two options that we spent some time looking at were meant to help us with mathematical equations and some of the charts and graphs that we may want to create if we are using the Python language. With that in mind, it is time to move on to a different library that can still prove to be really useful when you work on Python. This library is known as SciPy and it is going to be a good Python approved library that works more for technical and scientific computing.

When you take a look at the SciPy library, you will notice that there will be a ton of modules that are found inside. Some of the modules that are found in this library will include ODE solvers, image and signal processing, FFT< special functions, interpolation, integration, linear algebra, optimization, and many other modules that are going to make it easier to do tasks of engineering and science.

As you can imagine, there are a lot of different modules and more that are going to fit in with this idea, which is what makes the SciPy library a great one to work with. This library is going to build upon the NumPy array object, and it is going to be included in the same stack of NumPy as matplotlib. This should tell you that you are likely to use SciPy at some point if you are already working with the other two libraries as well.

SciPy is also going to be distributed using the BSD license, and it has a development that has been sponsored, as well as supported, by a community of developers who work to keep it nice and open for others to use. You will also find that this library is going to be supported by NumFOCUS, which is a community foundation that has the goal of supporting reproducible and accessible science, especially in Python.

When you decide to download the SciPy library or the package that goes with it, you will find that there are going to be a number of key functions and algorithms that are going to be included in this. This is done to help Python expand out some of its computing capabilities to work more in the scientific world. Some of the sub packages that are included with this library, if you choose to use them, will include options like:

Weave. This is a good tool to work with if you would like to write out C and C++ as Python multiline strings.

Stats: This is a function to deal with statistics.

Special: This is going to include any of the special functions that are included in this library.

Spatial: This is going to include a lot of the different machine learning algorithms that you will want to work with including distance functions, nearest neighbors, and KD-treas.

Sparse: This one is good for sparse matrix and some of the algorithms that are related to it.

Signal: This is going to be a signal processing tool.

Optimize: This is going to use some algorithms that are meant for optimization, including some that have to do with linear programming.

Ndimage: This one is going to be useful to the programmer who wants to work with various functions that are meant for multi-dimensional image processing.

Misc: This is going to include some miscellaneous utilities such as image writing or reading.

Linalg: This one is a good option to work with when you are trying to do some things with linear algebra routines.

Lib: This is a wrapper from Python that helps with some of the external libraries that you are trying to do.

Io: This is a good extension that you can use when it comes to data input and output.

Interpolate: This is a good option when it comes to interpolation tools.

Integrate: This is a good extension to use when it comes to numerical integration routines.

Fftpack: discrete Fourier transforms algorithms.

Clusters: This is another example of working with machine learning when you are doing the SciPy library. This is a good one that you can bring out when you want to do some of the machine learning algorithms like K-means, vector quantization, and hierarchical clustering.

Constants: And the final extension that we are going to take a look at is going to be the physical constants and conversion factors that you can work with.

Now, when you are working with some of the data structures that are used by this library, you will see that the most basic of this is going to be the multidimensional array that it is able to take from the module of NumPy. Since it is going to be associated back with NumPy, you will be able to use some of the random number generations, Fourier transforms, and even some functions that work with linear algebra. But the SciPy is able to take this a bit further because it is going to help with equivalent functions in a way that the NumPy library is not able to do.

You may also find that the NumPy library is going to be used in order to provide us with an efficient container of data that is multidimensional and is able to deal with data types that are arbitrary. The reason that this is so important is that it allows the NumPy library to work in a seamless manner to integrate with a lot of different databases, no matter what you are trying to work with.

In many cases, the older versions that you may have of SciPy would use Numeric as the point where it could get its array type. Of course, this has changed since Numeric is no longer using, and the NumPy array code is the one that the newer and more updated types of SciPy are going to be able to use.

There is a lot that you are going to be able to get when you use the SciPy library rather than some of the other options out there. It is a great way to expand out what you are able to do with the Python code, especially when it comes to numbers and using it for various scientific and engineering kinds of uses. There are also many extensions that come with this, which makes it the perfect addition to consider when you want to work with some types of machine learning, engineering, and even with some scientific options.

Scikit-learn

And the final library that we are going to take a look at is going to be the Scikit-learn library. This is going to be free software that you can use, and it has been designed to specifically help out with machine learning with the help of the Python language. So, if you are going to do some kind of project or coding that needs to work with machine learning, this is definitely one of the libraries that you need to take the time to download and learn how to use.

When we take a look at this library, you will find that it includes a ton of different options with it, especially when it comes to machine learning. You will be able to find a lot of clustering algorithms, regression algorithms, and classification algorithms. This is a lot of information, but some of the algorithms that you are the most likely to use with machine learning and find beneficial will include things like DBSCAN, k-means, gradient boosting, random forests, and support vector machines. These all come together to help you do a lot of the machine learning work that you want while relying on the Python code to make it easier to work.

This kind of library is also going to work so that you can add in the SciPy and the NumPy libraries that we talked about before. This way, if you need to bring in some formulas that are more numerical or more scientific, you will be able to integrate all of these in together as well. You may find, especially if your end goal is to write some codes that are more about machine learning than anything else, that downloading all three of these libraries is going to be the best option to help you get things done.

For the most part, the Scikit-Learn library is going to be written out in Python, which makes machine learning easier for a lot of people. There are going to be a few of the core algorithms though those have been written out with the Cython option in order to help achieve the performance that you are looking for. For example, you may see that the support vector machines are going to be implemented with the Cython wrapper attached to it.

As we have mentioned a bit in this section so far, the Scikit-Learn library is going to be based on the idea that many programmers are going to want to work with machine learning. This is a newer type of coding that has really taken off because it opens up the door to a lot of different types of programming that we may not be able to do with just Python on its own. This makes it highly adaptable and will ensure that we are able to make programs that keep up with the technology that is being offered now.

Let's look a bit at what machine learning is here. There is a lot that goes with this type of technology, and it is beyond the scope of this guidebook to talk about this in detail. But a little exploration will help us to get a better idea of what we are able to do when it comes to this library.

Machine learning is basically a type of programming that is going to teach the computer program how to make decisions and learn on its own. There are times when it is impossible for the coder to go through and figure out what all the answers will be based on their user. They just can't do it all because of the complexity of the program. And because of this, they are going to turn to some of the algorithms that are found in machine learning to make this work.

The best way to see how this works is to look at some examples of it. If you have ever used a search engine, then machine learning is something that is right at your fingertips. The program is able to look at your search query and pull up some of the answers and results that it thinks are the best. Over time, it starts to learn what kinds of results you like to get and will make better predictions.

Voice recognition software, like what we find on computers, or even on some of the different products like the Amazon Echo, are going to use this machine learning as well. The coder is not able to go through and guess what the user is going to say all the time or their speech patterns. So the device is programmed in order to learn from mistakes and get better at recognizing what the user is telling it.

These are just a few of the examples of what you will be able to do when it comes to the idea of machine learning. And the Scikit-Learn library is going to have some of the different algorithms that you need to use in order to make these things happen. Downloading it will be the best way to ensure that you are able to set yourself up for the best results with doing some of your own machine learning.

There are a lot of different parts that come with the Scikit-learn library, and since it is going to be attached to machine learning so much, there is going to be a lot of parts that we may not be able to explore as a beginner. With that said, we need to first take a look at the API that comes with this kind of library. The API of this library is designed to have a few different guiding principles in mind to help it work, including:

Consistency: All of the objects that are on this program need to be able to share a common interface. This interface is going to be drawn from a limited set of methods, but the documentation needs to be consistent between them.

Inspection: All of the values that are specified for the parameter are going to be exposed as attributes that are public.

Limited object hierarchy: Only the algorithms that are going to be represented by Python classes. The datasets are going to be represented in a standard format. And then the names of the parameters that you use will be found as a standard string in Python.

Composition: Many of the tasks that you try to use in machine learning are going to be used and expressed more as a sequence of the fundamental algorithms. The Scikit-Learn library is going to try and use this idea as often as it can.

Sensible defaults: When the models that you are working with need to have a user specify the parameters, the library is going to try to step in and define the default value that is the most appropriate to use here.

The idea with this one is that all of these principles are going to make sure that this particular library is as easy to use as possible, once you have the chance to understand some of the basic principles. Each of the algorithms for machine learning that is used in this library is going to then be implemented with the help of the Estimator API. The reason that this one is used is that it is able to provide a consistent interface for these algorithms, while offering room for all of the different applications of machine learning to be used.

This is a great thing because it is going to save you a lot of time. As you work with machine learning, you will notice that there are many different applications that work with machine learning. And if you had to change up the interfaces that you were able to do with each one all of the time, this would be a big hassle. This interface can handle many, if not all, of the machine learning algorithms that you are going to work with, which is really going to make a difference in the results that you get, and how easy it is to work with machine learning on the Python code.

All of these libraries are going to be great options to work with. They add in some new functionality to what you are able to do with Python, making it easier to work on some of the different types of programming that you want to do with Python, even if the original Python program isn't set up to do them. You may find that adding in a few of these libraries to your program and learning how to use the algorithms and more that come with them can add in a bit more functionality to the codes that you are writing and can make it easier for you to really get the results that you need out of some of your written programs.

Conclusion

Thank for making it through to the end of Learning Python, let's hope it was informative and able to provide you with all of the tools you need to achieve your goals whatever they may be.

The next step is to start working on some of the different codes and options that we have presented in this guidebook. You will find that there are a lot of different things that you are able to work on, and the options are just going to be limited based on the kind of programming that you want to do. This guidebook went over a lot of different parts of the Python code so that you are prepared and have a full understanding of how the Python code is going to work, and how you are able to write the codes that are found inside.

This guidebook is meant to be a great introduction to working with the Python language. There are a lot of parts that come in, and many times a beginner is going to look at is all and be worried that they don't understand how it works, or that they will never be able to code at all. But with some of the examples and exercises that we explored in this guidebook, you will find that even some of the more complex parts of the code are going to be easier to handle, and you will be able to use those as ways to really write some of your own code along the way.

When you are ready to learn a bit more about the Python language and how you can use some of the aspects of this language to write your own codes, make sure to check out this guidebook to learn exactly how to get it done!

If you found this useful you could also like:

PYTHON MACHINE LEARNING
Discover the Essentials of Machine Learning, Data Analysis, Data Science, Data Mining and Artificial Intelligence Using Python Code with Python Tricks

By Samuel Hack

I would like to thank you for reading this book and if you enjoyed it I would appreciate your review on Amazon!

www.ingramcontent.com/pod-product-compliance
Lightning Source LLC
Chambersburg PA
CBHW052146070326
40689CB00050B/2339